SNAKES
LONG LONGER LONGEST

by Jerry Pallotta
and Van Wallach

Illustrated by
Shennen Bersani

SCHOLASTIC INC.

New York Toronto London Auckland Sydney Mexico City New Delhi Hong Kong Buenos Aires

Thank you to Melissa Thompson and Donna Lawson
— Jerry Pallotta

To my parents with love, Elise June Zimmerman McNeil and Chester William McNeil
— Shennen Bersani

ISBN 0-439-83126-1

Text copyright © 2006 by Jerry Pallotta.
Illustrations copyright © 2006 by Shennen Bersani.
All rights reserved. Published by Scholastic Inc.
SCHOLASTIC and associated logos are trademarks and/or registered
trademarks of Scholastic Inc.

12 11 10 9 8 7 6 5 4 3 2   6 7 8 9 10 11/0

Printed in the U.S.A.

First printing, May 2006

Snakes are cold-blooded reptiles that have no arms and no legs. They have forked tongues. They have no ears and no eyelids. They can't blink. They are covered with dry scales.

Which snakes are long, longer, longest? Let's read and find out.

one inch

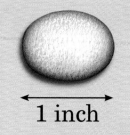

← 1 inch →

Which snake is the longest? Here is a brown-snake egg.
Look: It is one inch long. An inch is a unit of measurement.

one foot

Another unit of measurement is a foot. Twelve inches is equal to one foot. This ruler is twelve inches, or one foot, long. One rat snake is peeking out. It just hatched.

Three feet is equal to one yard. A yard is also 36 inches long. A flying snake is about three feet long. It sucks in its belly, spreads its ribs, steers with its tail, and glides from tree to tree.

A mile is 5,280 feet long or 1,760 yards long. No snake is a mile long. But a sea snake can easily swim a mile. All snakes can swim. This yellow-bellied sea snake and other sea snakes live in the Pacific Ocean and swim their whole lives.

The longest snake is a reticulated python. One was found that measured 32 feet 9 inches long! It is the longest snake ever recorded. It looked like this:

Long, longer, longest. This amazing reticulated python is about as long as a school bus. It would take more than a few friends to pick it up.

We can divide snakes into two categories. There are poisonous snakes, which have venom. And there are nonpoisonous snakes, which do not have venom. The longest venomous snake is the king cobra. It can grow to be eighteen feet long.

The tiny, tinier, tiniest venomous snake is the Dampierland burrowing snake.
It lives in Australia. An adult is only eight and a half inches long.

Heavy, heavier, heaviest. Which snake is the heaviest? The anaconda is the heaviest snake. It can weigh as much as five hundred pounds! You could not pick it up without help.

Light, lighter, lightest. The lightest snake
is also the most traveled. Flowerpot snakes travel around
the world. They hide in the soil of flowerpots people give to one
another. They weigh less than one ounce.

Wide, wider, widest. Width is a measurement too. The anaconda is the widest snake. It is wider than this nine-inch book. Like all snakes, it gets even wider when it eats something. An anaconda can swallow a whole pig. Anacondas even eat alligators!

Skinny, skinnier, skinniest. The blunt-headed tree snake is skinny like a pencil. Tree snakes have extra-long tails for balancing while moving among branches.

Fast, faster, fastest. Which is the fastest snake? A black mamba. It can really move! It can travel at twelve miles per hour. That is faster than most kids can run. An Olympic sprinter runs about twenty-seven miles per hour.

Slow, slower, slowest. The slowest snake is the wart snake. It hardly ever moves. Even its blood flow is slow. Its heart only beats once every two minutes.

Some people hate snakes. Some people love snakes. Most snakes are harmless. This is a Baja California mountain king snake. It is not poisonous. This snake is so friendly that some people keep it as a pet.

Some snakes are deadly! Here is a horned viper. It lives in the desert. In no time, this nasty snake could bite you, inject poison, and kill you. Yikes!

Most snakes are brown to blend in with the ground they crawl on. But snakes also come in a rainbow of colors. Do you know the colors of the rainbow? Red, orange, yellow, green, blue, indigo, and violet.

SNAKE COLORS

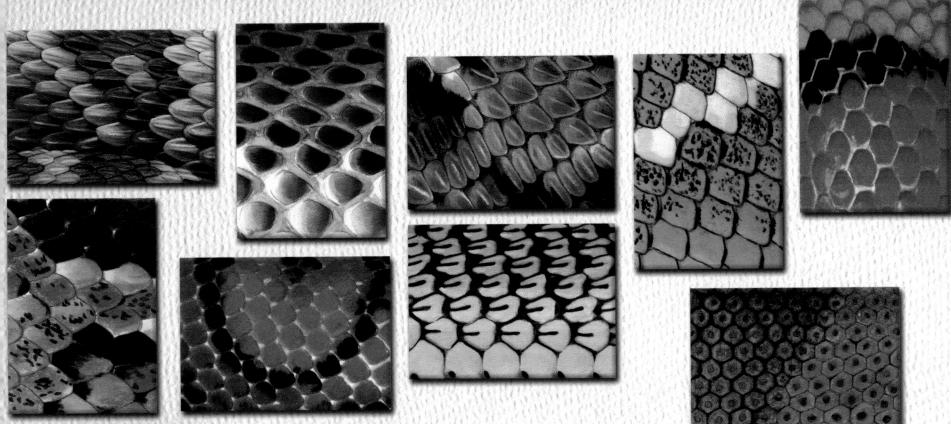

Snakes have scales on their skin. Some snakes have smooth scales and some have bumpy scales. The scales overlap and are neatly arranged. Many snakes have wild designs on their scales.

Snakes have long teeth in the front of their mouths called fangs. The Gaboon viper has the longest fangs. They are about two inches long. Snakes use their fangs to inject venom. Can you imagine how people would look with fangs?

Snakes also have a mouth full of small, pointy teeth. Their teeth are designed to catch food and hold it. A file snake has 110 teeth. The African egg eater only has six teeth.

Oops, this must be a mistake. Who put this snake jigsaw puzzle here?
This page is supposed to be "snake anatomy." Where are the body parts
of a snake?

This is better!
Here are the parts of a snake.

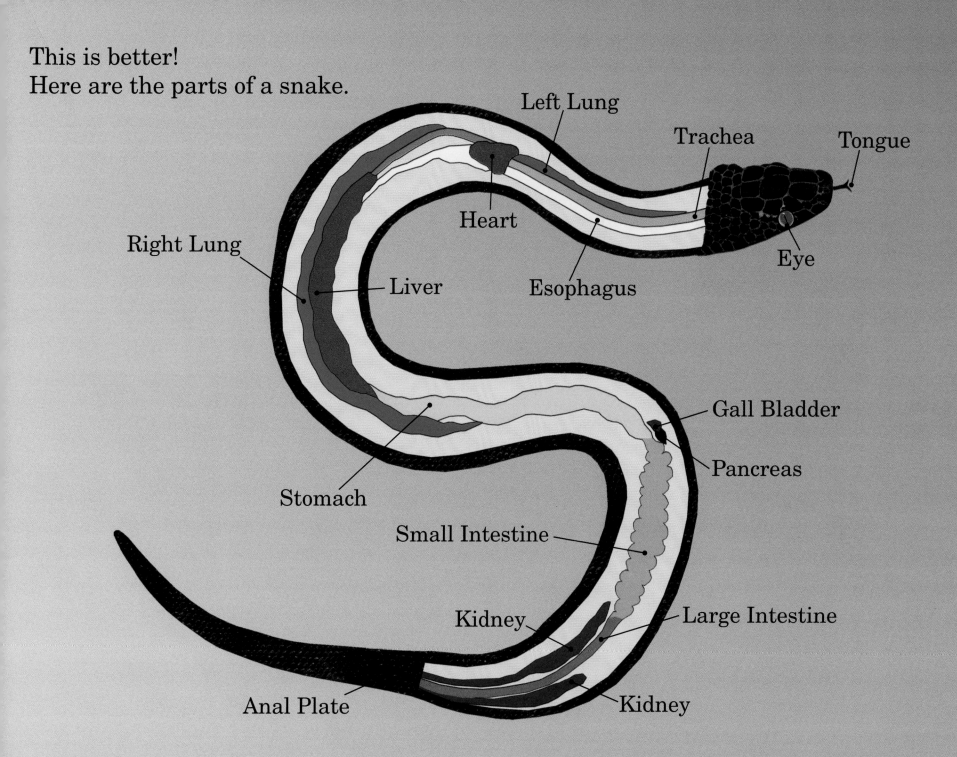

Snakes have organs like other animals except for one thing. Snakes do not have a bladder. It is amazing. Snakes poop, but they do not pee!

Snakes lay eggs in a clutch. A clutch might be hidden away in a small cave, in underbrush, or in a rotted log. A baby snake born from an egg is called a hatchling.

Not all snakes lay eggs. This mother garter snake has just given birth to a lot of baby snakes. Luckily, this mom does not have to buy shoes for all her babies.

People have round eyeballs and round pupils. Most snakes have round pupils. But some snakes have vertical pupils. Scary! Some have horizontal pupils. Spooky!

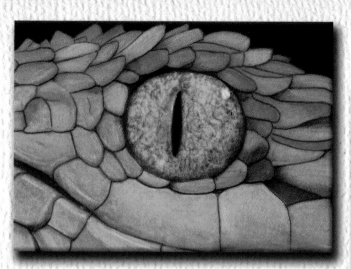

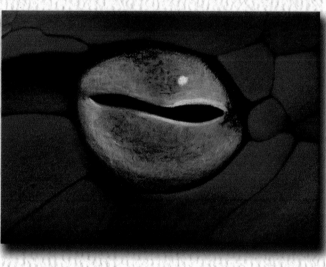

Spooky, spookier, spookiest.
Which one is your favorite snake eye?

Tasty, tastier, tastiest. Snakes do not chew their food. Snakes swallow their food whole. A lot of snakes are picky eaters. Some eat just snails. Others only eat crabs. How about only eating frogs, slugs, crickets, spiders, ants, centipedes, fish eggs, or scorpions? There is even a snake that just eats bats.

California king snakes eat everything they can catch. They even eat rattlesnakes! They would not eat a person because they could not swallow one whole. If you were a snake, what would your favorite food be?

We hope you enjoyed the snakes in this book.
We have one more surprise for you. Here is a
very rare two-headed milk snake. It was caught
in Maine. It has two names: Brady and Belichick.